Poetry
'From the Light'
for Your Inner Self

The first book in the 'From the Light' Series

Poetry Inspired by
My Visit with the White Light

Written and Illustrated by
Mary Theresa

Balboa Press books may be ordered through booksellers or by contacting:

Balboa Press
A Division of Hay House
1663 Liberty Drive
Bloomington, IN 47403
www.balboapress.com
844-682-1282

ISBN: 978-1-9822-7357-6 (sc)
ISBN: 978-1-9822-7358-3 (e)

Library of Congress Control Number: 2021917680

Print information available on the last page.

Balboa Press rev. date: 10/05/2021

BALBOA.PRESS
A DIVISION OF HAY HOUSE

Introduction
My Visit with the White Light

In the summer of 2015, as I was driving to work one morning, a car came into my lane and hit me head on!

The next thing I knew, I was floating in a space of pure, white light. Surrounded by a feeling of unconditional love enveloping me, I found myself, now in spirit form, gently moving forward toward a group of spirits some distance away. This line of spirits was waving to me and welcoming me, encouraging me to come join them.

It was at that instant when I realized I was in spirit form and in the White Light, that immediately thoughts of my kids and grandkids filled my heart. Just then, as I was thinking about the ones I love most, my spirit stopped, and no longer moved forward. Through this entire interlude with the White Light, my movements were being directed by another force, enabling me to realize that I was not controlling any part of what was happening to me or anything around me. As my spirit began to float to my right, there appeared before me three spirit beings. They were very close to me, unlike the row of spirits that were at a distance, also suspended in the light, and I was paused before them. I heard them say to me in a loving and kind voice, "you can stay with us, or you can go back, you have a choice." Still thinking of my kids and grandkids, I answered that I wanted to go back. Upon that declaration, my spirit again moved back to my previous stance with the line of spirits far away, and I began to move backwards.

But just as soon as I did, I began questioning my decision. I started reflecting about how beautiful this place was and the complete feeling of unconditional love that I was privileged to be a part of, and I really didn't want to leave. Abruptly, my spirit stopped again, and I heard the same voice of kindness repeat the exact same words, "you can stay with us or you can go back, you have a choice," but this time with a definite tone of, 'you must make up your mind!' A feeling of humility came over me, and I answered that I wanted to go back to be with my loved ones.

And so, here I am.

There is much more to this story and my White Light experience that I will be sharing with you soon in my 'From the Light' series of books; including some incredible things that have happened since my return, as well as beautiful revelations that I continue to receive. There was a great deal of inspiration that filled my heart as I returned to earth. I also knew that they, the spirits I encountered in the White Light, that I now call my spirit guides, would always be with me, guiding me in thriving to fulfill their goal of helping and inspiring others. I am truly blessed and humbled to be able to have this ongoing communication with the spirits of the White Light!

But for now, I am relaying this event so those who read my writings and poetry, will understand that the inspiration for the words and messages I impart, come from the direction of and with blessings from, the White Light.

This book is an introductory collection of poetry from some of the many subjects I have been inspired to put into writing and reveal to you. I have intuitively composed thousands of poems as of this writing, and several books, that as I mentioned, will be shared with you as I continue to publish messages from the White Light.

Within a week or so after surgery following the accident, I was released from the intensive care recovery unit at the hospital and sent to a rehabilitation center to begin the physical healing process, including learning to walk again. An unrelenting urge and what almost felt like a physical ache burned within me to write down words that were floating in my head. When my daughter brought me a notebook and pen that I requested, here is what emerged.

As I began writing, I immediately realized that although the poem was being written in the first person, the words were not mine, they were coming directly from the White Light!

A Moment of Pure Love
The Living White Light

Oh Light Divine, Oh Pure White Light,
my heart still yearns for you.
One moment of fear, and then of love,
a gift that cannot be explained, all new.

Peaceful warmth, and endless love,
yet words are far from clear.
A selfless cloud of faithful joy
allows my return to here.

An impossible task to share it now,
when understanding cannot be understood.
Eternal living light, a circle of love
awaits my soul for good.

2015

Dedication

This book is lovingly dedicated to my dear late friend and spiritual mentor, Ana.
Her unconditional love and guidance were the catalyst to these writings,
and her never-ending encouragement has brought me insights and inspiration
that would not have been possible without her.

I am also so very thankful to my spirit guides from the White Light for being a constant
inspiration, and who continue to share insights with me, for which I am eternally grateful!

"Everyone has their own personal belief system.
My strongest belief is that everyone has
a right to their own beliefs."

Inspirational Thoughts
'From the Light'

"If we can discover the stillness within, unconditional love is waiting for us."

"In the White Light, there is a reunion of souls."

"Illumination feels like being home."

"Strength comes from doing, not from thinking."

"When the inner Light is found, the darkness is no longer."

Table of Contents

CHAPTER ONE

Messages from the White Light

One God

It is said that there are many paths
to the one we call the Creator.
A single God for all mankind,
to find with our soul as navigator.

Many a door will open for us
as our destiny begins to take hold.
We search within our sacred selves,
as the ancient sages foretold.

The outside world at times reveals
being cold and selfish with hate.
We fight our battles inside and out,
affecting this journey and our fate.

Insight comes when surrender we fight
to our massive ego that rules.
If we allow it the power it craves,
we succumb to become and remain its fools.

These many roads are for us to seek
personal paths for inner peace.
They guide us to inspiration within;
serenity comes when conflicts cease.

Our goal is oneness, immortal and bright,
a pureness of essence yearning to unite.
The journey of spirit toward eternal light,
one God, one Spirit, one Living White Light.

Peace in Life and the Afterlife

We struggle each day with our human desires,
strange is our time that in so many hours,
through all of these moments we're unable to be
at peace with ourselves and others we see.

We can't seem to learn the beauty of peace,
lack of tranquility makes dread increase,
the everyday chaos that is ours, we live,
quite clearly shows the unrest we give.

So when the day comes that transition is here,
and we move on to the afterlife we fear,
the total peace of the Living White Light
will engulf our spirit with harmony and delight.

If we could only strive to attain
a stillness within to ascertain
that true serenity can teach the soul how
to have a moment of peace on this earth right now.

"The afterlife is timelessness sewn into the fabric of Pure Love."

A Second Chance for Salvation

Every so often as I'd go through my day,
I'd meet someone and feel I needed to say
how I had entered into the White Light,
and came back here with a blessed insight.

Reactions were upbeat, and did not rationalize,
except for one which came by surprise.
After revealing my secret to someone I met,
he volunteered his story with considerable regret.

A wound of war had caused him to die,
as he rose above his body, he was horrified.
Then, as he was cold and felt all alone,
he realized he was reaping the seeds he had sown.

He begged to go back and promised to change,
he feared this place, and was so ashamed
of how he had lived up until now,
and knew he needed to repent somehow.

The next thing he knew he was back and inspired,
in pain and aware of what had transpired.
He tells me he's trying to make amends,
his previous life, he no longer defends.

He said he was envious, but understood
how his experience changed him for good.
I wished him well as we went separate ways,
and he told me he'd see me at the end of our days.

The loving White Light had been denied that day,
he was in a place he did not want to stay.
They let him come back, and in his own way,
he was touched by the Light that saved him that day.

"The heir of my past is the future me."

The Warmth of the Light

Surrounded by a light of warmth, gentle and unconditional love,
a feeling of joy overtakes the known, eternal peace with God above.

Spirit consumed with a sacred rest, being invited to stay and be one,
with every spark of light now home, a new kind of life has just begun.

A Living Light encompassing all, where all is living and eternity calls,
a love extended to every being, forever waiting without any walls.

A Living White Light, so warm and calm, where gathering spirits confirm the divine,
welcoming with glee as all arrive, each and every soul at its time.

It seems that every once in a while, a choice is given to stay or go back.
I had that choice and returned to earth, with a directed purpose to give and pay back.

While feeling the warmth of a love unknown, is a glorious vision to have and behold,
where an endless light is pure and warm, a place where beauty finds a new threshold.

*"Peacefully rest in the knowledge
of the brilliance of the Living White Light."*

Intertwined with the Light

It may have been brief,
though time did elude
the Light in its presence,
yet my soul was renewed
with the mystery explained,
and filled with gratitude.

The uniting, divine,
humbling, yet warm,
touched by the Light,
with a flowing freeform,
unspoken thoughts, still understood,
a mystical journey to transform.

A joining of love,
interwoven and blessed,
mysteries shared,
inspiration expressed.
Intertwined with the Light;
insights granted to become manifest.

Living God's Glory

Now as my days become shorter, I see
the life I have lived, brings peace to me.
I never gave in to negative ways
or chose revenge throughout my days.

This physical life is here to teach
our soul to grow and His presence to reach.
I have been blessed from beginning to end,
was even allowed earthly barriers to transcend.

These writings are blessings so I can share
the gifts I've been given and to declare
the splendor of God and the pure delight
of encountering His glory in the Living White Light!

Near Death Experiences
(NDE's)

Recently, I've read where scientists can now explain,
what really happens when people think they died and came back again.

"NDE's are not spiritual at all, they can be biologically defined,"
researchers remark as if they are sure, with quite a closed frame of mind.

Scientists think their latest reveal, is surely the answer today.
Just as they did the very last time, and the time before that, now filed away.

Science cannot explain everything, such as, after we take our last breath.
Well, let me tell you they are amiss, they won't understand until death.

No one knows what they don't know, an open mind seems wise.
Intellect can only take us so far, beyond this life is a glorious prize.

It's just like so many other things, until you face it alone,
you can't understand experiences that you haven't had on your own.

Those of us who were blessed to be there, and in the White Light in His midst,
know for sure what happened was real, this place in the mist does exist.

"Sometimes when we lock a door, we forget the combination."

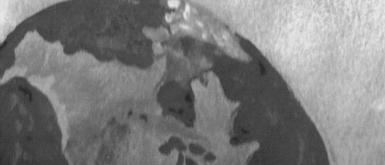

CHAPTER TWO

Poetry for Spiritual Growth

How to Pray for God's Help

We've all said a prayer sometime in our life
asking for God to assist us and such.
A specific help that we needed just then,
or maybe to seek a change in a rush.
Each petition, conclude by praying, His will be done,
as we may not know God's plan for us.

As Jesus instructed in the Lord's prayer,
"Thy will be done," is the secret key.
Imploring God's help with humility,
improves success consistently.
Reverence should need no clarification,
and *can* lead to an epiphany.

Wandering with Purpose

As I lazily saunter the sand-covered beach,
my mind begins to wander and reach
far-away places only dreamed of,
seeking to find an oasis to love.

I can imagine with my internal eye,
a quiet place in which to lie
on a billowy cloud of marbling white,
searching for a secret site.

As I awaken from my daydream conceived,
the waves tickle my toes interweaved
into the mush of the sand now cool,
quenching the thirst of life's daily school.

My spirit is lifted as I come back to earth,
knowing the gift and its special worth
of wandering in my mind for peace,
having created a mystical masterpiece.

"If we do not receive an answer to our prayers, maybe we are asking the wrong question."

A Strong Spirit

Have a young and vibrant sense of being,
one whose life is constantly seeing
opportunities that can be freeing.

Live a life of purposeful goals,
embrace your many personal roles,
to positively influence innumerable souls.

In this lifetime you can find
yourself to be warm, caring and kind,
and create a tranquil peace of mind.

Be strong in spirit and wisely be
a moral role model for all to see,
and rewards shall be given numerously.

Be the best example for all involved,
always forgive in order to resolve,
and use this lifetime for your soul to evolve.

Dawn of a New Light
(Meditation Enlightens)

A place of peace, of quiet delight,
waits for me each morning and night,
in solitude, yet never alone,
fills my spirit with love unknown.

In endless space, where no space exists,
my grateful heart has gently been kissed,
seeing the light and feeling its love,
brings my soul to a threshold above.

Deep inside the movement begins,
energy flowing on graceful wings,
a hidden passage opens to reveal
new thought patterns no longer concealed.

A radiant light is present and strong
nothing confusing, nothing wrong,
every sense is on high alert
making an impact, a lovely concert.

Message received, as the flow dissipates,
knowing I will return to this glorious state,
a moment of bliss while in total peace,
a new light dawns that is now in reach.

"Meditation is the map for finding your way back home."

Climbing Upward

An uphill battle appears is here,
the end result is not clear.
How does the light enter my sphere
when now my life is defined by a tear?

I had a dream of climbing out,
I was not sure, full of doubt,
if I could ever escape without
losing myself in this morality drought.

All was bleak, seemed useless to try,
easier to languish, easier to cry,
much of my life is such a lie,
how can I grow while I still deny?

Facing myself was hardest though,
but once I did, I seemed to know
the answer was always what path to hoe,
as what I reap, I must sow.

Stairs to climb with steps quite slim,
hard to maneuver with light so dim,
I must keep climbing, though things look grim,
to reach the top as I climb the rim.

Mountains high, past clouds of grey,
opening up to a bright new day,
troubles weigh, but I do not betray
my faith for a new triumphant pathway.

The Rejoining
Returning to the Source

As we are born into this challenging world,
our soul enters into its test.
It begins to try to improve itself
to relieve its burden of unrest.

We stumble upon a self-weakness,
temptations arise and immediately,
we try to deny these feelings inside,
and ignore them with no modesty.

Our soul-searching brings our fear to a head
and confronts our failings face to face.
Its honesty clashes with unresolved pride,
and tests our resolve to its base.

Our soul yearns within, to return once again
to its source for peace to reveal
a silent yet beautiful place within reach,
where harmony and calm it will feel.

If we persist to grow peace in our hearts,
then in eternal tranquility immerse,
the rejoining can be within our grasp,
as we advance toward the source.

CHAPTER THREE

Virtues, the True Test of Character

A Tear in the Fabric of Morality

Many things seem insignificant at first
and not worth the attention deserved,
intolerance, hate, lust and lies,
are often dismissed when observed.

Ethics demand we act certain ways
distinguishing wrong from right,
our values determine our actions direct,
and should also influence us in hindsight.

Principles apply to everyone,
no matter their status or age,
if we sit back and do nothing to stop it,
we are as wrong as them, to not engage.

Nowadays there is so much crime,
with abuse everywhere you look,
in numerous forms and in many ways,
so our virtues must be an open book.

We cannot live in our safe cocoon,
ignoring the world outside,
for when we are judged, as will be the case,
strength of character will be verified.

To Understand Virtues

Compassion is often an elusive goal,
how can empathy even console?
Kindness and caring are used to explain
compassion in ways that we cannot retrain
our minds to deploy to be helpful somehow,
it often hasn't worked, before or now.

Patience is mostly an on-going test,
perseverance is needed in order to invest
in building endurance in long term trials
where resistance is simply fierce denials.
How can we, expect to be patient, when insistence
only brings more pressure for persistence?

Humility is another unachieved virtue,
our pride is real, and we surely prefer to
hold on to our ego, though mostly scorned,
yet we can't say we haven't been duly warned
that we could use some modesty traits,
something to work on, the challenge awaits.

Love incorporates virtue attained,
concern for others, with caring unrestrained.
The only way to learn love at its best
is to practice loving, unrepressed.
The same applies to virtues at large,
open your heart so love may take charge.

11

Attaining

How do we attain the wisdom of virtues?
When we begin to apply a much broader view.
To distinguish righteousness and thereby learn
how to behave and to always discern
just how to manifest these in our lives,
in dealings with others till insight arrives.
Mercy, faith, and kindness, are gifts of the divine,
the benefits of these qualities can truly shine.
Only by being and manifesting same,
can we then attain virtues acclaimed.

The Beginning of Wisdom

There is only one reason for wisdom to seek,
for the assisting of others is the only technique.
A virtue of helping should always be strong
as we influence others, teaching right over wrong.
Highlighting their virtues, and not their faults,
is the beginning of wisdom coming out of the vault.

Ask Not

Ask not for powers or gifts for oneself
only for wisdom to know thyself.
Advancement will come as He allows,
and with humility, His mercy endows.

"We are all connected, so when we hurt others, we hurt ourselves."

Love Can Build a Bridge

Things have changed, a relationship stalled,
after many a year, a friend is called,
advice is requested on how to repair
a damaged heart, because we still care.

A friendship is challenged by diverse points of view,
not previously discussed, so the reaction is new.
Strong opinions expressed from both did bruise,
after speaking words of anger from opposite views.

There is a secret that's no secret at all.
Delve into the heart and break down the wall,
dividing you from where you know you belong,
build it with love, and the bridge will be strong.

The Umbrella of Kindness

*A virtue is a gift to ourselves as we
patiently practice high moral standards.
These traits of character deem us to be
kind and gracious to all bystanders.*

*Courage and honesty deserve thankfulness,
faith and gratitude ensure reverence.
Patience with fairness honors gentleness,
while loyal commitment brings excellence.*

*Each of these exhibit supreme foresight,
yet one humbly stands above the rest.
When kindness is present, all is right,
allowing us to manifest acts that are best.*

*Compassion and caring show selflessness,
as we hope discernment proves to be just.
So once we employ an umbrella of kindness,
all other virtues take shelter in trust.*

Truth is Truth

Truth is truth, then and now, it does not change no matter how
the world may shift, and then see from a point of view, differently.
Not through time, not through space, not with cultures and not with race.
Always the same, even if creeds differ in understanding or needs.
Truth cannot change, it is what it is, though different beliefs may often exist,
conveying attitudes of the current times, yet a basic truth cannot be maligned.

Our evolution has allowed us to bring new insight to teachings of the King,
who lived on earth in times of old, still the message remains as it was told.
Societies' policies sometimes preach their own set of truths to try to reach
the people of whom they wish to control and to that end no real truth is sold.
Whether preached or sung or just believed, doctrines and rules are often conceived
in good faith, but that does not mean that one's understanding is Truth as it seems.

Morality changes as do virtues admired, a judgement of self must be required.
How can we judge others when they behave, in a way that they feel *their* soul craves?
So just be careful of transient schemes, they come and go like the wind in a dream.
We must be steadfast, faithful and pure, so our inner guidance can lead us for sure.
Find a peacefulness deep inside, live in peace with a humble pride,
knowing the true Truth is within, as it always has been, now and then.

"The Truth of the universe is permanent and unalterable."

CHAPTER FOUR

Poetry for the Senses

First Light

Eyes still closed with the mind still blurred,
yet inside our being a feeling has stirred,
a peaceful moment of silence preferred,
then the soft, lovely song of a robin is heard.

The chorus of dawn awakens the light,
it opens the morning and closes moonlight,
our awakening senses feel the sunlight
warming our face as our eyes bestow sight.

A tranquil time of soothing grace,
no matter the day, no matter the place,
a delicate layer of silk-like lace,
infusing our spirit with a tender embrace.

The glory of sunrise does not come by chance,
like the beauty of a kindling romance,
it showers our senses with its mystical trance,
and readies us for the first light's dance

Gazing Up Through the Four Seasons

Amid the damp, yet soft green grass,
I laid beneath a tree.
The fresh new air of spring warmed me,
as I peered upward, totally carefree.

New leaves were emerging from winter's hold,
while sparkling light shown through.
A newborn hatchling chirped for food,
my young mind knew this life was brand new.

Later that summer I stretched out to rest,
on my gentle safe spot so near.
My sun-kissed tree now full of blooms,
just waiting for fruit to appear.

As it shaded my brow with sweat now cooled,
I shielded my face with my cap.
The summer heat had blistered my feet,
then I dozed off and took a nap.

As the blustery winds blew chilly that day,
I lay on the crumbly fall leaves,
surrounded by an enchanting scene,
I harvested the apples like thieves.

Looking up from my bed of crisp sounds,
I watched the falling of leaflets break down,
and shower me with golden tears,
like pieces of gilded paper burned brown.

Snowfall now covers my pasture of peace,
while snow-angels form engaging my arms.
The winter-grey skies peak through the limbs
of my ice-covered tree and its naked charms.

I'll never forget that tree in the field
where peacefully I lay many times.
Sheltered while maturing, as if it knew
that we both were growing…in our seasoned lifetimes.

A Moist Morning Meadow

I slowly stroll in the morning mist,
as the first light of dawn peaks through,
hugging the muted layered horizon,
while melting the fresh morning dew.

A soft light creeps across the growth,
from far away it sneaks
toward the budding yellow meadow
dancing atop its valleys and peaks.

A peaceful place where sound is shy
with only the flutter of wings,
so the air can capture the magic of
all the mystical, morning things.

The moisture lingers just long enough
for the trance to be lifted, to teach
the meadow how to come to life,
so enchanted dreams are still in reach.

Floating on a Melody

The notes of a melody ring true in my ear,
while the rhythm and tempo play as I hear
a gentle set of sounds so soft and clear,
filling my eyes with a single tear.

So moved is my soul that all it can do
is silently wait and listen for a clue
to move itself closer and eventually through
the magical myriad of dreams to pursue.

Wavy encircled bubbles of sound
float through impressions circling around,
gurgling upstream while reflections abound,
filling the senses as if magically found.

Drifting on air as a tune takes shape,
but never solidifies its reason or drape
of numerous colors trying to escape
the untamed melody's musical landscape.

God's Green Valley

Lush green meadows filled with flowers abloom,
a waterfall streaming alongside a log flume,
tall mountain peaks covered with snow,
watching over the beauty of the valley below.

Down in the valley cabins coexist
peacefully with all of nature's gifts,
a blending of numerous majestic sights
resting in solitude through the cool nights.

Aromas of fresh leaves fill the glen
while billowy clouds float time and again,
plateaus of boulders keep bighorn sheep
safe from the elements while predators sleep.

High from the summit magnificent views
are seen by the eagles as they soar in the blue,
reaching heights that only they can;
all of this beauty given from God to man.

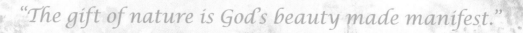

"The gift of nature is God's beauty made manifest."

CHAPTER FIVE

Socially Conscious

Secret Lives
(Same sex partnerships)

When secret words
are not meant to be heard,
yet a little bird
has overheard,
and creates the absurd.

Behind the door fear awaits,
it brings ignorance and diverse hates.
It's truly a shame that same sex mates
aren't allowed in all states,
our tolerance, however, waits.

Truth comes through,
and no one knew
the other view,
or what one would do
if it were you.

So now it's known,
and you feel so alone.
You need not think you must atone.
Your heart does moan,
and needs repair and must be sewn.

Words alone cannot bring relief,
as now the hurt is so deep.
Your secret will not keep.
Your private life has taken a leap,
now you'll sow in order to reap.

Society's changing as time goes by,
it now whispers words that do not lie,
while the chosen ones keep asking why,
yet letting the couples breathe a sigh,
that the time for acceptance is finally nigh.

2020, The Lost Year

Totally unprepared were we
for the Covid nightmare that came to be.
Like a thief in the night, it snuck right in
leaving us perplexed as to how to begin
to fight this unknown mystery strain
of a virus so deadly, fear still remained,
as new variants continued to appear
threatening health again the following year.
Twenty-twenty was a painful time,
so many suffered and many died over time.
Yet, at the same time, time was illusive,
it wasn't pleasant and not conducive
to achieving anything meaningful, it seemed,
though through it all we nevertheless dreamed.
We challenged ourselves and learned to be
alone while together in the cloud, you see.
We looked inside and found ourselves
strong and able, so inwardly we delved.
Some were lost, yet many were found,
a few soaring above, others earthbound.
Experiences faced were difficult at best,
some overcame and others needed rest.
We strive to restore happier times, and to return
to calmness, without viral concern.

Welcome to the Earth

What has become of the forests and trees?
There used to be so many of these,
but fires and floods have taken them away
and we wonder if we'll have them back someday.

What has become of the oceans so blue?
They used to be clean and with species anew,
but now our litter and plastics kill
much of the aquatic life, even still.

Wildlife has lost their land and domain,
as houses are built and where sidewalks remain.
Searching for food, into trashcans they break,
dying alone, while empathy we fake.

The polluted air makes it hard to breathe,
industrial waste is what we leave.
How can we say we've tried our best,
when the earth cries out, you're only a guest!

Violence

Our world today is violent and cruel.
Vicious thoughts, bring brutal duels.

Our streets are not safe, and it's a disgrace,
we fear for our lives, cause there's no safe place.

From early-on our children are shown,
to carefully weigh who they trust and have known.

Questionable is loyalty and hope,
because we have doubts if we can cope.

Guns are prolific on each leg and waist.
Hidden from sight and licensed in haste.

Society worldwide is struggling with fear.
Our spirits are damaged, yet commitment sincere.

But what are we doing as we commence,
we continue to kill, with global offense.

All we can reason is to stay alive.
We fight and attack, struggling to survive.

We must look within and forget the dark past.
The sooner we do, the easier surpassed.

Do we not realize that when we have hate,
it's really ourselves creating our own fate?

We can't seem to grasp that when we are done,
there's no escape, as we are all one.

In soul and in time, connected are we.
We think we can run from our linked destiny.

If we look deep inside, we can indeed understand,
how the future is lost if we fight on demand.

So instead of a challenge to someone out there,
let's challenge ourselves to share and to care.

"It is in rigidity that violence occurs."

What If?

We have such beauty to enjoy every day,
our forests have giant redwoods on display,
birds sing and fly and go on their migrating way,
traveling to safety and shelter far, far away.
We have waters that flow and animals that play,
even as the sun provides light and warmth every day.

But...

What if the oceans were void of life?
What if the skies displayed no flight?
What if the lands were barren overnight?
What if our forests began to ignite?
What if the sun was no longer bright?

What if the mountains were out of sight?
What if our pastures were condemned with a blight?
What if our deserts had sands like a knife?
What if the jungles had no sun light?

What if our pets could no longer delight?
What if wildlife were endangered due to oversight?
What if the storms brought anguish and plight?

What if there were no more starlight?
What if the answer was out of sight?

What if our earth were hit with a meteorite?

Instead...

What if we envisioned to have foresight,
to ensure we don't have to regret in hindsight?

What if we have some positive insight?
Safeguard and maintain while we reunite.
Conserve, preserve and shelter while forthright.

If we observe, admit, and begin to highlight,
concede that nothing can happen overnight,
then decisions we make will keep our birthright.
We must save our planet, producing a green light!

CHAPTER SIX

A Medley of Inspiration

The Autumn of My Life

As I slowly walk along
a colorful winding road,
the autumn leaves are falling still
with yellows, oranges, greens and gold.

A crisp coolness fills the air,
as evening finds it way
into the now dimly lit path,
as trampled leaves fly away.

My feet have not kept up the pace
of last year's autumn stroll,
and now I reach my destination
later than my earlier goal.

It really doesn't matter when
I get home to lay me down,
and ease into my easy chair,
allowing sleep to come around.

Autumn remains the respite before
a long and cold winter is here,
and so my body prepares itself,
as life reflects the cycles of the year.

Before the dead of winter takes hold
my thoughts, as the leaves, turn to Fall,
deep into a mysterious place
where the seasons tend to stall.

My Butterfly Garden

Flutters of wings capture the air,
lifting their colors with artistic flair.
Having escaped from the cocoon's lair,
now are free to fly here and there.

So many beauties grace our lands,
in meadows and forests and spacious wetlands,
where swallowtail thrive with the help of mans' hands
and many species conservation demands.

I so love my garden in the warm sunlight,
I savor its beauty and tend it at night,
aromas fill my soul with delight,
as butterflies seem to gather in flight.

Colorful wings of blue, orange and green.
Marbling and spotted, with stripes that gleam,
sparkle in moonlight and wink at the queen,
some are bright blue and others tangerine.

Monarchs rule in this magical place,
crystal clear Glasswings shine in light like lace,
where flowers and butterflies join with grace,
to share their habitat in this colorful showcase.

My butterfly garden, so peaceful at dawn,
brings tranquil thoughts, while morning looks on.
Serenity lies where gazes are drawn,
in my butterfly garden nature smiles upon.

*"Once we develop our vision to observe,
we will see the glory of all creation."*

Until

Until the earth is silent,
until the rain never falls,
until the land is barren,
and the birds cease their calls.

Until the sun no longer shines
and this world flies off into space,
until my very last breath is taken,
I'll hold you in my loving embrace.

I Will Be the One

I will be the one that holds on tight,
I will be the one that will hold you in the night.
I will be the one that will never judge,
I will be the one who will not need a nudge.
I will be the one who will surely let you in,
I will be the one who will encourage you to win.
I will be the one that will forever comfort you,
I will be the one that will be there when you're blue.
I will be the one who will always lift you up,
I will be the one who makes sure you have enough.
I will be the one to brush the tears away,
I will be the one who will never leave, and forever stay.
I will be the one who will be there anytime,
I will be the one who will cherish you
your whole lifetime.

Love has Love

Love has meaning when you're loved,
a mutual warmth with your beloved.
Love is simple, yet it is hard,
it should never have to be on guard.
Love has no agenda at its best,
surrounded by caring and feeling blessed.

Love has poise and patience with each other,
and especially respect for one another.
Love has trust between the two,
so do not lie to avoid an adieu.
Love does not have vanity or pride,
humility is always your safest guide.

Love does not expect or presume,
it should never judge or assume.
Love has highs and love has lows,
it's the way it is, and so it goes.
Love has no selfishness inside,
when a giving nature is identified.

Love, if it's real, cannot be crude,
anything uncivil should not intrude.
Love has no envy, it should always feel
that understanding embraces a moral ideal.
Love comes in all sizes and every shape,
wear it with kindness like a beautiful drape.

A Moonlight Sail
The Savior Light

An evening sail we planned, on a cool but restless night,
we sailed just after dinner, into the pale moonlight.

With romance on our mind, we failed to check the weather,
all we could think about was an enchanting evening together.

Our magical time was special, but as the stars appeared,
clouds moved in quickly and the moonlight disappeared.

The wind began to howl and caution we needed to heed,
we turned around and started back, at a much faster speed.

A fog rolled in and through the mist, no object could be seen,
the storm's violent dominance was like a monster machine.

The waves were strong and forceful, rocking the boat so much,
that we feared we would capsize without a God-sent touch.

We couldn't see the shore, when a bright light appeared beaming,
and through the fog we hurried, as the ray of the light kept gleaming.

The bent-over caretaker came to visit, talking about the lighthouse tale,
he'd known the light was broken and felt so bad during the gale.

We told him our remarkable story of how we saw the light,
it guided us to safety, on that cold and stormy night.

The town has now renamed the lighthouse since that day,
it is fittingly called the 'Savior Light,' and a plaque is now on display.

We often sit and silently watch, as others sail at night,
but now we're daytime sailors, saying thanks to God for the miracle searchlight.

Printed in the United States
by Baker & Taylor Publisher Services